THE DOCTRINE OF THE HEART

THE DOCTRINE OF THE HEART

BY
ANNIE BESANT

GYAN

ISBN: 978-81-212-1892-4 (HB)
First Published, 1920
Published, 2018
Published by

Gyan Publishing House
5, Ansari Road
Daryaganj, New Delhi-110002
Phone: 011-47034999, 9811692060
www.gyanbooks.com
E-mail: books@gyanbooks.com

Printed at: G. Print Process, Delhi.

FOREWORD

LEARN to discern the real from the false, the ever-fleeting from the ever-lasting. Learn, above all, to separate Head-learning from Soul-wisdom, the "Eye" from the "Heart" doctrine.—*Voice of the Silence.*

UNDER the title of THE DOCTRINE OF THE HEART are here printed a series of papers, consisting chiefly of extracts of letters received from Indian friends. They are not given as being of any "authority," but merely as containing thoughts that some of us have found helpful, and that we wish to share with others. They are intended only for those who are resolutely seeking to live the Higher Life, and are addressed to those especially who know that this life leads to a definite entering on the Path of Discipleship under the

Great Ones who trod it in the past, and who remain on earth to help others to tread it in their turn. The thoughts in these letters are thoughts that belong to all religions, but the phrases and the sentiment are Indian. The devotion is of that noble and intense kind known in the East as Bhakti—the devotion that surrenders itself wholly and unreservedly to God and to the Divine Man through whom God is manifest in the flesh to the devotee. This Bhakti has nowhere found more perfect expression than in Hinduism, and the writers of these letters are Hindus, accustomed to the luxuriant richness of the Sanskrit, and tuning the harsher English into some faint harmony with the poetical sweetness of their mother-tongue. The chill and reserved dignity of the Anglo-Saxon and his emotional reticence are wholly alien from the out-flowing of religious feeling that wells up from the Eastern heart as naturally as song from the lark. Here and there in the West we find a true Bhakta [devotee], such as S. Thomas à Kempis, S. Theresa, S. John of the Cross, S. Francis of Assisi, S. Elisabeth of Hungary. But for the most part, religious feeling in the West, however deep and true, tends to silence and seeks to hide itself. To those who shrink from the expression of religious feeling these letters will not be helpful, and for them they are not intended.

Let us now turn to the consideration of one of the marked contrasts of the Higher Life. We have all of us recognised the fact that Occultism makes on us demands of a character which necessitates a certain isolation and a rigid self-discipline. Both from our much-loved and revered Teacher, H. P. B., and from the traditions of the Occult Life, we have learned that renunciation and stern self-control are required from him who would pass through the gateway of the Temple. *The Bhagavad*

Gîtâ constantly reiterates the teaching of indifference to pain and pleasure, of the perfect balance under all circumstances, without which no true Yoga is possible. This side of the Occult Life is recognised in theory by all, and some are obediently striving to mould themselves into its likeness. The other side of the Occult Life is dwelt upon in *The Voice of the Silence*, and consists of that sympathy with all that feels, that swift response to every human need, the perfect expression of which in Those we serve has given Them as title "The Masters of Compassion." It is this, in its practical, every-day aspect, to which these letters direct our thoughts, and it is this which we overlook most in our lives, however much the beauty of it, in its perfection, may touch our hearts. The true Occultist, while he is to himself the sternest of judges, the most rigid of taskmasters, is to all around him the most sympathising of friends, the gentlest of helpers. To reach this gentleness and power of sympathy should, then, be the aim of each of us, and it can only be gained by unremitting practice of such gentleness and sympathy towards all, without exception, who surround us. Every would-be Occultist should be the one person, in his own home and circle, to whom everyone most readily turns in sorrow, in anxiety, in sin—sure of sympathy, sure of help. The most unattractive, the most dull, the most stupid, the most repellent, should feel that in him, at least, they have a friend. Every yearning towards a better life, every budding desire towards unselfish service, every half-formed wish to live more nobly, should find in him one ready to encourage and strengthen, so that every germ of good may begin to grow under the warming and stimulating presence of his loving nature.

To reach this power of service is a

matter of self-training in daily life. First we need to recognise that the SELF in all is one; so that in each person with whom we come in contact, we shall ignore all that is unlovely in the outer casing, and recognise the SELF seated in the heart. The next thing is to realise—in *feeling*, not only in theory—that the SELF is endeavouring to express itself through the casings that obstruct it, and that the inner nature is altogether lovely, and is distorted to us by the envelopes that surround it. Then we should identify ourselves with that SELF, which is indeed ourself in its essence, and co-operate with it in its warfare against the lower elements that stifle its expression. And since we have to work through our own lower nature on the lower nature of our brother, the only way to effectually help is to see things *as that brother sees them*, with his limitations, his prejudices, his distorted vision; and thus seeing them, and being affected by them in our lower nature, help him in his way and not in ours, for thus only can real help be given. Here comes in the Occult training. We learn to withdraw ourselves from our lower nature, to study it, to feel its feelings without being thereby affected, and so while emotionally we experience, intellectually we judge.

We must utilise this method for our brother's help, and while we feel as he feels, as the synchronised string gives out the note of its fellow, we must use our disengaged "I" to judge, to advise, to raise, but always so using it that our brother shall be conscious that it is *his* better nature that is uttering itself by our lips.

We must desire to share our best; not to keep, but to give, is the life of the Spirit. Often our "best" would be unattractive to the one we are trying to help, as noble poetry to a little child; then we must give the best he can assimilate, withholding the other, not because we grudge it, but because he does not yet want it. Thus do the Masters of Compassion help us who are as children to Them, and in like fashion must we seek to help those who are younger than we are in the life of the Spirit.

Nor let us forget that the person who happens to be with us at any moment is the person given to us by the Master to serve at that moment. If by carelessness, by impatience, by indifference, we fail to help him, we have failed in our Master's work. We often miss this immediate duty by absorption in other work, failing to understand that the helping of the human soul sent to us *is* our work of the moment; and we need to remind ourselves of this danger, the subtler because duty is used to mask duty, and failure of insight is failure in accomplishment. We must not be attached even to work of any particular description; always at work indeed, but with the soul free and "at attention," ready to catch the slightest whisper from Him, who may need from us service of some helpless one whom, through us, He wills to help.

The sternness to the lower self, spoken of above, is a condition of this helpful service; for only the one who has no cares of his own, who is for himself indifferent to pleasure and pain, is sufficiently free to give perfect sympathy to others. Needing nothing he can give everything. With no love for himself, he becomes love incarnate to others.

In Occultism the book of life is the one to which we turn our chief attention. We study other books merely in order that we may live. For study even of Occult works is only a means to spirituality if we are striving to live the Occult Life; it is the life and not the knowledge, the purified heart, not the well-filled head, that leads us to our Master's Feet.

The word "devotion" is the key to all true progress in the spiritual life. If in working we seek the growth of the spiritual movement and not gratifying success, the service of the Masters and not our own self-gratulation, we cannot be discouraged by temporary failures, nor by the clouds and deadness that we may experience in our own inner life.

To serve for the sake of service, and not for the pleasure we take in serving, is to make a distinct step forward, for we then begin to gain that balance, that equilibrium, which enables us to serve as contentedly in failure as in success, in inner darkness as in inner light. When we have succeeded in dominating the personality so far as to feel real *pleasure* in doing work for the Master which is painful to the lower nature, the next step is to do it as heartily and fully when this pleasure disappears and all the joy and light are clouded over. Otherwise in serving the Holy Ones we may be serving self—serving for what we get from Them, instead of for pure love's sake.

So long as this subtle form of self-seeking prevails, we are in danger of falling away from service if darkness remain long around us, and if we feel dead inside and hopeless. It is in this night of the spirit that the noblest service is rendered, and the last snares of the lower self are broken through.

We lay this stress on devotion, because everywhere we find that aspirants are endangered, and the progress of the Master's work is hindered, by the predominance of the personal self. Here is our enemy, here our battle-ground. Once seeing this, the aspirant should welcome everything in his daily life that chips a bit off the personality, and should be grateful to all the "unpleasant persons" who tread on his toes and jar his sensibilities and ruffle his self-love. They are his best friends, his most useful helpers, and should never be regarded with anything but gratitude for the services they render in bruising our most dangerous enemy. Looking thus on daily life, it becomes a school of Occultism, and we begin to learn that perfect balance which is required in the higher walks of discipleship, ere deeper knowledge, and therefore power, can be placed in our hands. Where there is not calm self-mastery, indifference to personal matters, serene devotion to work for others, there is no true Occultism, no really spiritual life. The lower psychism demands none of these qualities, and is, therefore, eagerly grasped at by pseudo-Occultists; but the White Lodge demands these of its postulants, and makes their acquirement the condition of entrance into the Neophytes' Court. Let the aim of every aspirant be, therefore, to train himself that he may serve, to practise stern self-discipline that "when the

Master looks into the heart He may see no stain therein." Then will He take him by the hand and lead him onward.

ANNIE BESANT.

THE DOCTRINE OF THE HEART

DISASTER hangs over the head of the man who pins his faith on external paraphernalia rather than on the peace of the inner life, which depends not on the mode of the outer life. In fact, the more untoward the circumstances, and the greater the sacrifice involved by living among them, the nearer does one come to the final goal from the very nature of the trials one has to overcome. It is unwise, therefore, to be attracted too much by any outward manifestation of religious life, for anything that is on the plane of matter is ephemeral and illusive, and must lead to disappointment. Anyone who is drawn powerfully to any external modes of living has to learn sooner or later the comparative insignificance of all outer things. And the sooner one passes through experiences necessitated by past Karma the better it is for the individual. It is unwelcome indeed to be suddenly thrown off one's ground, but the cup which cures folly is ever bitter, and must be tasted if the disease is to be eradicated. When the gentle breeze coming from Their Lotus Feet blows over the soul, then you know that the worst external surroundings are not powerful enough to mar the music that charms within.

Just as a European who is drawn to Occultism feels nearer to the Great Ones when he lands in India, so does an Indian feel when he ascends the heights of his snowy Himavat. And yet it is quite an illusion, for one approaches not the Lords of Purity by physical locomotion, but by making oneself purer and stronger through constant suffering for the welfare of the world. As for the ignorance of the poor deluded world regarding our revered Lords, I am reminded of the words: "The hissing of the serpent does more harm to the sublime Himavat, than the slander and abuse of the world to any of us."

*
* *

If it be once admitted, as it must be by all who have any knowledge of Occultism, that there are hosts of invisible agencies constantly taking part in human affairs, Elementals and Elementaries of all grades breeding all sorts of illusion and masquerading in all garbs, as well as members of the Black Lodge who delight in gulling and deluding the votaries of true wisdom—one must also recognise that Nature, in her great mercy and absolute justice, must have endowed man with some faculty to discriminate between the voices of these aërial denizens and that of the Masters. And I fancy that it will be agreed on all hands that reason, intuition and conscience are our highest faculties, the only means by which we can know the true from the false, good from evil, right from wrong. That being so, it follows that nothing which fails to illuminate the reason and satisfy the most scrupulous claims of the moral nature should ever be regarded as a communication from the Masters.

It must also be remembered that the Masters are the Masters of Wisdom and Compassion, that Their words illumine and expand, never confound and harass the mind; they soothe, not disturb; they elevate, not degrade. Never do They use methods which wither and paralyse reason and intuition alike. What would be the inevitable result if these Lords of Love and Light were to force on Their disciples communications revolting equally to the reason and the ethical sense? Blind credulity would take the place of intelligent faith, moral palsy instead of spiritual growth would ensue, and the Neophytes would be left quite helpless, with nothing to guide them, constantly at the mercy of every frolicsome nymph, and worse still, of every vicious Dugpa.

Is this the fate of discipleship? can such be the way of Love and Wisdom? I do not think that any reasonable man can believe it for any length of time, although for a moment a glamour may be thrown upon him and he may be made to swallow the veriest absurdities.

*
* *

AMONG the many doubts thrown into the mind of the disciple to cause him distress, is the doubt whether physical weakness may be a bar to spiritual progress. The process of assimilation of spiritual nourishment involves no drain upon physical energies, and spiritual progress can go on while the body suffers. It is an entire fallacy, due to lack of knowledge and of balance, to suppose that the torture and starvation of the body make it responsive to *spiritual* experiences. It is by doing that which best serves the purpose of the Holy Ones that steady and real progress is made. When the right time comes for spiritual experiences to be impressed on the brain-consciousness, the body cannot stand in the way. The little difficulty that can be raised by the body can be swept away in a second. It is a delusion that any physical effort can advance spiritual progress by a single step. The way to approach Them is to do that which best furthers Their wish, and this done, nothing else needs to be done.

* * *

It seems to me that there is a peculiar sweetness in being resignedly patient, in gladly sacrificing one's own will to the will of Those who know better and always guide aright. There is no such thing as personal wish in the life of the Spirit. So the disciple may gladly sacrifice his own personal bliss, while They find occasion to work through him for others. He may sometimes feel as though forsaken when he is alone, but he will always find Them at his side when work has to be done. Periods of night must alternate with those of day, and it is surely well that darkness should come at a time when it affects ourselves alone, even though our personal pain should be thereby intensified. To feel Their presence and influence is indeed the divinest gift imaginable, but even that we should be willing to sacrifice, if by renouncing what we deem the highest and best, the final good of the world be made easier of attainment.

* * *

TRY and realise the beauty of suffering, when suffering only makes one better fitted for work. Surely we can never crave for peace if in strife the world must be helped. Try and feel that though darkness seems to be all round you, yet it is *not* real. If They sometimes veil Themselves in an outer Mâyâ of indifference, it is but to shed Their blessings with greater luxuriance when the season is ripe. Words avail not much when the darkness is overshadowing, yet the disciple should try to keep unshaken his faith in the nearness of the Great Ones, and to feel that though the light is temporarily withdrawn from the mind-consciousness, yet, under Their wise and merciful dispensation, it is growing daily within. When the mind again becomes sensitive, it recognises with surprise and joy how the spiritual work has gone on without its having had any consciousness of the details. We know the Law. In the spiritual world nights of greater or less horror invariably follow the day, and the wise one, recognising the darkness to be the outcome of a natural law, ceases to fret. We can rest assured that the darkness, in its turn, will lift. Remember always that behind the thickest smoke is ever the light from the Lotus Feet of the Great Lords of the earth. Stand firm and never lose faith in Them, and there is then nothing to fear. Trials you may, and indeed must, have, but you will be sure to withstand them. When the darkness that hangs like a pall over the Soul lifts, then we are able to see how really shadowy and illusive it was. Yet this darkness, as long as it lasts, is real enough to bring ruin to many a noble soul that has not yet acquired strength enough to endure.

* * *

SPIRITUAL life and love are not exhausted by being spent. Expenditure only adds to the store and makes it richer and intenser. Try and be as happy and contented as you can, because in joy is the real spiritual life, and sorrow is but the result of our ignorance and absence of clear vision. So you should resist, as much as you can, the feeling of sadness;

it clouds the spiritual atmosphere. And though you cannot entirely stop its coming, yet you should not altogether yield to it. For remember that at the very heart of the universe is Beatitude.

* * *

DESPAIR should find no room in the heart of the devoted disciple, for it weakens faith and devotion, and thus furnishes an arena for the Dark Powers to wrestle in. The feeling is a glamour cast by them to torture the disciple, and if possible to reap some advantage for themselves out of the illusion. I have learned from the bitterest experience that self-reliance is quite unavailing and even deceptive under trials of this nature, and the only way to escape unscathed from these illusions is to devote oneself completely to Them. The reason of this, too, is plain enough. The force, in order to be effective in its opposition, must be on the same plane as that on which the power to be counteracted plays. Now as these troubles and illusions come not from the self, the self is powerless against them. Proceeding as they do from the Dark Ones, they can only be neutralised by the White Brothers. Therefore it is necessary for safety to surrender ourselves—our separated selves—and to be freed from all Ahamḳâra.

* * *

KNOWING as we do that our Society[1]—or, for the matter of that, every movement of any consequence—is under the watch and ward of vastly wiser and higher Powers than our little selves, we need not concern ourselves much about the ultimate destiny of the Society, but rest content with doing our duty by it conscientiously and diligently, playing the part assigned to us according to our best light

[1] The Theosophical Society

and abilities. Care and solicitude have, no doubt, their own functions in the economy of Nature. In ordinary men they set the brains to work, and even the muscles to motion, and were it not for these the world would not make half the progress it has done on the physical and intellectual planes. But at a certain stage of human evolution these are replaced by a sense of duty and a love of Truth, and the clearness of vision and impetus to work thus attained can never be furnished by any amount of molecular energy and nervous vigour. Therefore shake off all despondency, and with your Soul turned towards the Fountain of Light work on to that great end for which you are here, your heart embracing all mankind, but perfectly resigned as to the result of your labours. Thus have our Sages taught, thus did SHRÎ KṚIṢHṆA exhort Arjuna on the battle-field, and thus shall we direct our energies.

My own feelings with regard to the sufferings of the world are precisely the same as yours. There is nothing which pains me more than the blind and frantic manner in which a vast majority of our fellow-beings pursue the pleasures of the senses, and the utterly blank and erroneous view they take of life. The sight of this ignorance and madness touches my heart much more tenderly than the physical hardships that people undergo. And although Rantideva's noble prayer moved me deeply years ago, with the glimpse that I have since been allowed into the inner nature of things, I regard the Buddha's sentiments as wiser and more transcendental. And though I would gladly suffer agony to relieve a disciple of the torture to which he is subjected, yet having regard to the causes as well as the intimate consequences of a disciple's sufferings, my grief for them is not half so intense as it is for the misery of those ignorant wretches who *unintelligently* pay the mere penalty of their past misdeeds.

* * *

THE functions of intellect are merely comparison and ratiocination; spiritual knowledge is far beyond its scope. You are probably quite surfeited with intellectual subtleties in your present surroundings; but the world is, after all, only a school, a training academy, and no experience, however painful or ridiculous, is without its uses and value to the thoughtful man. The evils that we come across only make us wiser, and the very blunders we make serve us in good stead for the future. So we need not grumble at any lot, however outwardly unenviable.

* * *

KARMA, as taught in the *Gîtâ* and the *Yoga Vâsishṭha*, means acts and volitions proceeding from Vâsanâ, or desire. It is distinctly laid down in those ethical codes that nothing done from a pure sense of duty, nothing prompted by a feeling of "oughtness," so to say, can taint the *moral nature* of the doer, even if he be mistaken in his conception of duty and propriety. The mistake, of course, has to be expiated by suffering, which must be proportionate to the consequences of the error; but certainly it cannot degrade the character or tarnish the Jivâtmâ.[1]

* * *

It is well to use all the events of life as lessons to be turned to advantage, and the pain caused by separation from friends we love may thus be used. What are space and time on the plane of the Spirit? Illusions of the brain, nonentities merely, acquiring a semblance of reality from the impotency of the mind, the involucra which imprison the Jivâtmâ. The suffering merely gives a fresh and more potent impulse to live altogether in the Spirit.

[1] The individualised Self.

Good will come in the end to every one of us out of the pain, and so we must not murmur. Nay, knowing that to disciples nothing of any consequence can happen which is not the will of their Lords, we must look upon every painful incident as a step towards spiritual progress, as a means to that inner development which will enable us to serve Them, and hence Humanity, better.

* * *

If we can but serve Them, if through all storms and conflagrations our Souls turn to Their Lotus Feet, what matter the pain and the sufferings that these inflict on our transitory wrappings? Let us understand a little of the inner meanings of these sufferings, these vicissitudes of outer circumstances—how so much pain endured means so much bad Karma worked out, so much power of service gained, such a good lesson learned—are not these thoughts sufficient to support us through any amount of these illusory miseries? How sweet it is to suffer when one knows and has faith; how different from the wretchedness of the ignorant, and the sceptic, and the unbeliever. One could almost wish that all the suffering and misery of the world were ours, in order that the rest of our kind might be liberated and be happy. The crucifixion of Jesus Christ symbolises this phase of the disciple's mind. Do you not think so? Only be always firm in faith and devotion, and swerve not from the sacred path of Love and Truth. This is your part—the rest shall be done for you by the Merciful Lords you serve. You know all this, and if I speak of it, it is only to strengthen you in your knowledge; for we often forget some of our best lessons, and in times of trouble the duty of a friend is more to remind you of your own sayings than to inculcate new truths. Thus it is that Draupadî often consoled her sage husband Yudhisṭhira when dire misfortune would for a moment overthrow his usual serenity, and thus Vasishṭha himself had to be soothed and comforted when torn with the pangs of his children's death. Truly unspeakable is the Mâyâ side of this world! how beautiful and romantic on the one hand, and yet how horrible and wretched on the other. Yes, Mâyâ is the mystery of all mysteries, and one who has understood Mâyâ has found his own unity with BRAHMAN—the Supreme Bliss and the Supreme Light.

* * *

THE startling picture of Kâlî standing on the prostrate SHIVA is an illustration of the utility—the higher use—of Anger and Hatred. The black complexion represents Anger; with the sword it also means physical prowess; and the whole figure means that so long as a man has anger and hatred and physical strength he should use them for the suppression of the other passions, the massacre of the desires of the flesh. It also represents what really happens when first the mind turns towards the higher life. As yet we are wanting in wisdom and in mental equilibrium, and so we crush our desires with our passions; our anger we direct against our own vices, and thus suppress them; our pride also we employ against the unworthy tendencies of the body and mind alike, and thus gain the first rung of the ladder. The prostrate SHIVA shows that when one is engaged in a warfare like this, he pays no heed to his highest principle, the Âtmâ—nay, he actually tramples upon it, and not until he has slain the last enemy of his Self does he come to recognise his actual position during the fight with regard to the Âtmâ. Thus, Kâlî finds SHIVA at her feet only when she has killed the last Daitya, the personification of Ahamkâra, and then she blushes at her insane fury. So long as the passions have not all been subdued, we must use them for their own suppression, neutralising the force of one with that of another, and thus alone can we at first succeed in killing out selfishness, and in catching the first glimpse of our true Âtmâ—the SHIVA within us—which we ignore while desires rage in the heart.

* * *

WELL may we always lay aside our own short-sighted personal wish in order to serve Them faithfully; it is my experience that in thus following Their guidance alone one always avoids some dangerous precipice against which one was unconsciously running. For the moment it seems hard to break away from one's likings, but in the end nothing but joy results from such sacrifice. There is no training better than the few brief years of one's life when one is driven by sheer disappointment to seek shelter under the blessed Feet of the Lords, for nowhere else is there room for rest. And then there grows in the disciple a habit of thinking always that his only refuge is in Them, and whenever he thinks not of Them he feels miserable and forlorn. Thus from the very darkness of despair burns out for him a light that never afterwards grows dim. Those whose eyes penetrate the stretches of the far-off future, which are veiled from our mortal eyes, have done and will do what is best for the world. Immediate results and temporary satisfactions must be sacrificed, if the end is to be secured without a chance of failure. The stronger we desire to make the chances of ultimate success, the less should we crave for the reapings of the day. Only by pain can we attain to perfection and purity; only by pain can we make ourselves fit servants of the Orphan that cries incessantly for food spiritual. Life is only worth having as it is sacrificed at Their Feet.

LET us rejoice that we have opportunities of serving the great Cause by personal sacrifices, for such suffering can be used by Them to draw the poor erring Humanity a little step higher. Any pain that a disciple may suffer is an earnest for a corresponding gain that comes to the world. He should, therefore, suffer ungrudgingly and gladly, since he sees a little more clearly than the blind mortality for which he suffers. In the whole course of evolution there is one law that is only too painfully evident, even to the eyes of the merest tyro, that nothing that is really worth having can be obtained without a corresponding sacrifice.

* * *

HE who resigneth all sense of self, and maketh himself an instrument for the Divine Hands to work with, need have no fear about the trials and difficulties of the hard world. "As Thou directest, so I work." This is the easiest way of passing outside the sphere of individual Karma, for one who layeth down all his capacities at the Feet of the Lords creates no Karma for himself; and then, as SHRÎ KṚIṢHṆA promises: "I take upon Myself his balance of accounts." The disciple need take no thought for the fruits of his actions. So taught the great Christian Master: "Take no thought for the morrow."

* * *

Do not allow impulses to guide conduct. Enthusiasm belongs to feeling, not to conduct. Enthusiasm in conduct has no place in real Occultism, for the Occultist must be always self-contained. One of the most difficult things in the life of the Occultist is to hold the balance evenly, and this power comes from real spiritual insight. The Occultist has to live more an inner than an outer life. He feels, realises, knows, more and more, but shows less and less. Even the sacrifices he has to make belong more to the inner world than to the outer. In ordinary religious devotion all the sacrifice and strength one's nature is capable of are used in adhering to externals, and in overcoming ridicule and temptations on the physical plane. But these have to be used for grander objects in the life of the Occultist. Proportion must be considered, and the external subordinated. In a word, never be peculiar. As the Hamsa takes the milk alone and leaves the water behind from a mixture of both, so doth the Occultist extract and retain the life and quintessence of all the various qualities, while rejecting the husks in which these were concealed.

* * *

How can people suppose that the Masters ought to interfere with the life and actions of people, and argue for Their non-existence, or for Their moral indifference, because They do not interfere? Folk might with equal reason question the existence of any moral Law in this Universe, and argue that the existence of iniquities and infamous practices among mankind is against the supposition of such a Law. Why do they forget that the Masters are Jîvanmuktas and work with the Law, identify themselves with the Law, are in fact the very spirit of the Law? But there is no need to be distressed over this, for the tribunal to which we submit in matters of conscience is not public opinion but our own Higher Self. It is battle such as this that purifies the heart and elevates the soul, and not the furious fight to which our passions, or even "just indignation," and what is termed "righteous resentment," impel us.

* * *

WHAT are troubles and difficulties to us? Are they not as welcome as pleasures and facilities? For are they not our best trainers and educators, and replete with salutary lessons? Does it not then behove us to move more evenly through all changes of life and vicissitudes of fortune? And would it not be much to our discredit if we failed in preserving the tranquillity of mind and equilibrium of temper which ought always to mark the disposition of the disciple? Surely he should remain serene amid all external storms and tempests. It is a mad world this, altogether, if one looks at the mere outside of it, and yet how deceptive in its madness! It is the true insanity of lunacy where the subject of the disease is ignorant of his condition —nay, believes himself perfectly sound. Oh! if the harmony and the music which reign within the Soul of things were not perceptible to us, whose eyes have been opened to this utter madness that pervades the outer shell, how intolerable life would be to us.

Do you not think that it is not quite grateful to be cheerless, when we are obeying the wishes of our Lords and are out on our duty? You should not only have peace and contentment but also joy and liveliness, while you are serving Those whose service is our highest privilege and the memory of whom is our truest delight.

* * *

THAT They will never desert us is as certain as Death. But it is for us to cling to Them with real and deep devotion. If our devotion be real and deep there is not the remotest chance of our falling away from Their holy Feet. But you know what real and deep devotion means. You know just as well as I do that nothing short of complete renunciation of the personal will, the absolute annihilation of the personal element in man, can constitute Bhakti proper and genuine. It is only when the *whole* human nature is in perfect harmony with the Divine Law, when there is not one discordant note in any part of the system, when all one's thoughts, ideas, fancies, desires, emotions voluntary or involuntary, vibrate in response to and in complete concord with the "Great Breath," that the true ideal of devotion is attained, and not till then. We only rise beyond the chance of failure when this stage of Bhakti is reached, which alone ensures perpetual progress and undoubted success. The disciple does not fail through lack of care and love on the part of the Great Masters, but in spite of these, and through his own perverseness and inborn weakness. And we cannot say that perverseness is impossible in one who has yet lingering in him the idea of separateness—ingrained through æons of illusive thought and corruption, and not yet completely rooted out.

* * *

We must not delude ourselves in any way. Some truths are indeed bitter, but the wisest course is to know them and face them. To dwell in a fancied paradise is only to shut off the real Elysium. It is true that if we sit down deliberately to find out whether or not we have still any trace of separateness or personality left in us, any wish to counteract the natural course of events, we may fail to find any motive, any reason, for such self-assertion or wish. Knowing and believing as we do that the idea of isolation is a mere product of Mâyâ, that ignorance and all personal desires flow only from this feeling of isolation and are the root of all our misery, we cannot but scout these false and illusory notions when reasoning upon or about them. But if we analyse the actual facts, and watch ourselves all the day, and observe the various modes of our being, varying with the different circumstances, a very different conclusion will press itself upon us, and we shall find that the actual realisation in our own life of our knowledge and belief is yet a far-off incident and comes only for a brief moment now and again, when we are entirely forgetful of the body or any other material environment, and are completely wrapped in the contemplation of the Divine—nay, are merged in the Deity Himself.

* * *

To us, through the supreme mercy of our Lords, things on earth are a little plainer and more intelligible than to the man of the world, and that is why we are so eager to devote all our life's energy to Their service. All activity—charity, benevolence, patriotism, etc.—a cynic will say with jubilant sneer, is mere barter, is a pure question of give and take. But the nobler aspect which even this jeered-at, mercantile honesty—strictly construed and applied to higher walks of life—presents to the higher eye, is beyond the ken of the supercilious mocker; and so he laughs at and scouts honesty, calling it mercantile, and the foolish and light-hearted world, thirsting for a little mirth, laughs with him and calls him a shrewd and witty fellow. If we look at the surface of this wonderful sphere of ours, nothing but sadness and gloom will overspread our souls, and despair will paralyse all efforts at bettering its condition. But, looking beneath, how all inconsistencies melt away, and everything appears beautiful and harmonious, and the heart blooms and is gladdened, and liberally opens its treasures to the surrounding universe. So we need not feel disheartened at any frightful sight we see, nor mourn over the madness and the blindness of the men amidst whom we are born.

* * *

THERE are fixed moral laws, just as there are uniform physical laws. These moral laws may be violated by man, endowed as he is with individuality and the freedom which that involves. Each such violation becomes a moral force in the direction opposite to that towards which evolution is drifting, and inheres in the moral plane. And by the law of reaction each has a tendency to evoke the operation of the right law. Now, when these opposing forces accumulate and acquire a gigantic form, the reactionary force necessarily becomes violent and results in moral and spiritual revolutions, pious wars, religious crusades, and the like. Expand this theory and you understand the necessity for the appearance of Avatâras on earth. How easy things become when one's eyes are opened; but how incomprehensible they look when the spiritual vision is blind, or even dim and dull. Nature in her infinite bounty has provided man on the outer planes with exact facsimiles of her inner workings, and verily those who have eyes to see may see, and those who have ears to hear may hear.

How intense is the longing to carry aid to the suffering Soul, in its hours of dire trial and of dreary darkness. But experience shows those who have passed through similar ordeals, that it is well that they did not at such times perceive the aid that yet is always given, and that they were weighed down with a sad sense of loneliness and of being totally forlorn. Were it otherwise, half the effect of the trial were lost, and the strength and knowledge which follow every such ordeal would have to be acquired by years of groping and tottering. The law of Action and Reaction is everywhere operative. . . . One whose devotion is complete, *i.e.*, one who in deed as well as in thought consecrates all his energies and all his possessions to the Supreme Deity, and realises his own nothingness as well as the falsity of the idea of separateness—such a one alone is not allowed to be approached by the powers of darkness, and is protected from every danger to his Soul. The passage in the *Gîtâ* you are thinking of must be interpreted to mean that no one who has the feeling of devotion once awakened in him can fall away *for ever*. But there is no guarantee for him against temporary aberrations. Why, in one sense, every living being from the highest Angel to the meanest protozoon is under the protection of the LOGOS of his or its system, and is carried through various stages and modes of existence back to His bosom, there to enjoy the blessedness of Moksha for an eternity.

* * *

THE *without* always reveals the *within* to the seeing eye, and places and people are therefore always interesting. Again, the *without* is not such a despicable thing as one may fancy in the first intensity and acuteness of his Vairâgya, or disgust with shows. For if it were so, all creation would be a folly and a purposeless expenditure of energy. But you know that it is not so in fact; that on the other hand there is a deep and sound philosophy even in these illusory manifestations and outward vestures, and that Carlyle in his *Sartor Resartus* has shadowed forth a portion of this philosophy. Why then turn with sickness and horror from even the outermost garbage? Are not even the robes in which the Supreme Deity masquerades holy to us and full of wise lessons? You say rightly that all things, fair and foul, have their suitable places in Nature, and constitute by their very difference and variety the perfection of the Supreme Logos.

* * *

Why should communication with the inside world be cut off, causing sadness and heaviness of heart? Because the outside has still some lessons to teach, and one of these lessons is that it also is divine in its essence, divine in its substance, and divine in its methods, and that therefore you should take more kindly to it. On the other hand, sadness and melancholy have their use and philosophy. They are as much needed for the evolution and budding out of the human Soul as joy and liveliness. They are, however, needed only at the earlier stages of our growth, and are dispensed with when the Self has blossomed out and has opened its heart to the Divine Sun.

* * *

You know how evolution works. We begin with no sensation at all. Gradually we develope it, and at one point of our pilgrimage we have it in the intensest degree. Then comes a period in which sensation is looked upon as Mâyâ, and thus it begins to diminish and knowledge predominates, until in the end all sensation is burned up by knowledge, and we have absolute peace. But not peace in nescience, as at the commencement of our life in the mineral kingdom, but peace in omniscience—peace, not in complete apathy and as it were death, such as we see in stones, but in absolute life and absolute love. This finds rest, because it enlivens all that is, and pours its blessings upon the whole Universe. But extremes meet, and so in one of the aspects the beginning and the end coincide.

*
* *

Two points I want to make clear: (1) That untrained psychics always run the risk of putting forward things really said by the enemy as injunctions from the Master; and (2) That the Master says nothing that the intellect of His audience cannot grasp, and against which their moral sense revolts. Master's words, however much they may be opposed to one's previous thoughts, never fail to bring the most absolute conviction, alike to the intellect and to the moral sense of the person addressed. They come like a revelation, rectifying an error which becomes at once apparent; they stream down like a column of light dispelling the gloom; they make no claim on credulity or blind faith.

* * *

You know how the enemy has been working against us, and if we fail in our devotion to Masters, or in the discharge of the duties with which They have been pleased to entrust us, he will give us no end of trouble. But these troubles we do not much mind; we can endure them quite patiently and without a ruffle. What does torture us and disturb the peace of our mind, is the tearing away from our Lords with which we are now and again threatened. Nothing else can torment us—no personal pain, no physical loss, however great their amount. For we know beyond all doubt that all that is personal is transitory and fleeting, and all that is physical is illusory and false, and that nothing but folly and ignorance mourn over things belonging to the world of shadows.

*
* *

For the disciple little is gained from teaching on the intellectual plane. The knowledge that infiltrates from the Soul down into the intellect is the only knowledge worth having, and surely as the days roll by the disciple's store of such knowledge increases. And with the increase of such knowledge comes about the elimination of all that hinders him on the Path.

*
* *

The feeling of pain is one to which any person who leads the life of the Spirit becomes accustomed. We know that pain cannot last for ever, and even if it did it would not matter very much. We cannot hope to be of any service to Them or to Humanity without taking our full measure of suffering from the enemies. But the ire of these Monarchs of Darkness is sometimes terrible to face, and they perfectly startle one by the Mâyâ they sometimes create. But a pure heart has nothing to fear and is sure to triumph. The disciple must not distress himself over the temporary pain and illusion they try to create. Sometimes they may seem to work a regular havoc inside, and then he has to sit upon the ruins of himself, quietly waiting for the time when the âsuric Mâyâ shall pass away. Always he should allow the wave of doubt and unrest to sweep over him, holding firmly to the anchor he has found. The enemy can do him no real or substantial harm, so long as he remains devoted to Them with all his Soul and with all his might. "He who clingeth to Me easily crosseth the ocean of death and of the world, by My help."

* * *

NOTHING can happen to the disciple but that which is best for him. Once a person deliberately puts himself into the Hands of the gracious Masters, They see that everything happens at the proper time—the time at which the greatest advantage is reaped, alike for the disciple and for the world. He should therefore take all that comes in his way with a contented and cheerful spirit, and "take no thought for the morrow." . . . The storm-tossed bark on a raging sea is more peaceful than the life of the pilgrim to the shrine of Spirit. A peaceful life would mean stagnation and death in the case of one who has not acquired the right to peace by completely destroying the enemy—personality.

* * *

You should not fall into fallacies that are committed by the ignorant. All real Love is an attribute of the Spirit, and Prânâ and Bhakti are the two aspects of the Divine Prakriti (Nature) which go to make worth living the life of an aspirant after the waters of immortality. In the stormy darkness of the disciple's life the sole light comes from Love, for Love and Ânanda (Bliss) are in the highest sense identical, and the purer and the more spiritual the Love the more does it partake of the nature of Ânanda, and the less is it mixed with incongruous elements. Only the Masters' holy love is so majestically serene as to have nothing in it that does not partake of the Divine.

* * *

DISCRETION and economy are quite as necessary in Occultism as anywhere else. In fact, in the life of the Occultist all the faculties of the human mind that are regarded as virtues in the ordinary sense are put to the greatest use and exercise, and are necessary adjuncts to the real life which alone makes a disciple. The world cannot be helped so easily as many imagine, even if there were more agents available for the work. Knowledge on the part of the disciple is not the only thing needed. Look out and ponder, ere deciding that the knowledge and devotion of the few can push on the hands of the clock. Not a single attempt can be made without provoking fierce hostility from the other side, and is the world prepared to survive the reaction? You will understand how wise are our Lords in not going further than They do, if you only learn from all you have seen.

* * *

WHAT would life be worth if we did not suffer—suffer to render the world groaning under our eyes a little purer, suffer to win a little more of the waters of life that will quench the thirst of some parched lips? In fact, but for the suffering that is the fate of the disciple who walks with bleeding feet on the Path, he might stray away and lose sight of the goal on which his gaze must ever be fixed. The Mâyâ of the phenomenal world is so confusing, so bewitching, that it seems to me that the elimination of the pain must inevitably be followed by oblivion of the realities of existence, and with the disappearance of the shadow of spiritual life its light would vanish too. So long as man has not been transformed into God, it is vain to expect to be in uninterrupted enjoyment of spiritual bliss, and in periods of its absence suffering alone keeps the feet of the disciple steady, and saves him from the death which would surely overtake him in the forgetfulness of the verities of the spiritual world.

* * *

THE disciple should not be disturbed nor surprised when the spiritual forces turned against him by the other side find their playground on a plane higher than that of the physical intellect. It is true that the dying embers in some unseen and unnoticed cranny of his own nature may be fanned thereby into flame; but the flame is one that forms the signal of the final destruction of some weakness that must be burned away. So long as the taint of personality has not been clean washed out, vice in its manifold forms may find shelter in some neglected chamber of the heart, though it may not find expression in mental life. And the only way to render the sanctuary of the heart immaculate is to let the search-light pierce into dark crannies, and calmly witness the work of their destruction. The disciple must never let this purificatory process fill him with dismay, whatever monstrosities he may be called upon to witness. He must hold fast to the Feet of Him who dwells in the glorious burning-ground of all that is material; then he has nothing to fear or to be anxious about. He has faith in Those who protect and help, and may well leave the workings on the spiritual plane to be watched and directed by Them. When the dark cycle is over, he will again recognise how the gold shines when the dross has been burned away.

* * *

In this mundane sphere of ours, as on all planes of existence, night alternates with day—there is shadow beneath the lamp itself. And yet how strange that men of culture and erudition should fancy that with the advancement of Science, of gross materialistic Science, all misery, individual, racial, and national, will cease for ever and ever; diseases, droughts, plagues, wars, inundations, nay, cataclysms themselves will all be things of the remote past!

* * *

The interest that we have in all the affairs of this elusive sphere belongs only to the emotions and the intellect, and cannot touch the Soul. So long as we identify ourselves with the body and the mind, the vicissitudes which overcome the Theosophical Society, the dangers which threaten its life or solidarity, must have a depressing, nay, sometimes almost a frenzied, influence upon our spirits. But as soon as we come to live in the Spirit, to *realise* the illusory nature of all external existence, the changeful character of every human organisation, and the immutability of the Life within, we must, whether the brain-consciousness reflect the knowledge or not, feel an inward calm, an unconcernedness, as it were, with this world of shadows, and remain unaffected by the revolutions and eruptions of the world. Once the Higher Ego is reached, the knowledge that the Laws and Powers which govern the universe are infinitely wise becomes instinctive, and peace in the midst of outward throes is inevitable.

* * *

ROUGHLY and broadly speaking, on the plane we live upon there are three standpoints of looking at human misery in general. We may regard it, for instance:

(1) As a test of character; (2) as a retributive agency; and (3) as a means of education in the largest signification of that word. From all these points of view, I fancy the "deadness" (experienced by all aspirants at times) stands to acute pain in very much the same relation as solitary confinement to imprisonment with hard labour. The illustration is, no doubt, a very crude one, but it seems to me very suggestive, and I have invariably found analogy to be of great help in the comprehension of abstract and subtle propositions; hence this plan of explaining things. Again, all the forces here are working towards the evolution of perfected humanity, and it is only by the harmonious development of all our higher faculties and nobler virtues that we can attain perfection. And this harmonious development is possible only by the proper exercise of those faculties and virtues, while this exercise in its turn requires

particular conditions for each distinct attribute. *Positive* intense suffering does not either test or repay or bring into play the same capacities and merits of mankind as a dull, dreary void within. Patience, passive endurance, faith, devotion, are far better developed under a mental gloom than during an active, hard struggle. The law of action and reaction holds good on the moral plane, and the virtues evoked by this mental "numbness" are those best fitted to combat and overcome it; and these are certainly not the same with which you confront actual pain, however excruciating. One word more on this point, and I shall pass on. This state of mind indicates that the pilgrim is on the borderland between the known and the unknown, with a distinct tendency towards the latter. It marks a definite degree of spiritual growth, and points to that stage where the Soul in its onward march has vaguely, yet unmistakably, realised the illusive character of the material world, is dissatisfied and disgusted with the gross things it sees, and knows and hankers after things more real, knowledge more substantial.

The above explanation, though very succinct and desultory, will, I hope, satisfy you as to the utility of vairâgya—of the feeling of the absence of all life and reality in both yourself and the world around you—in the economy of Nature, and show how it serves as a touchstone for firmness of mind and singleness of heart, how as a punitive measure it antidotes intellectual egoism—the philosophical blunder of identifying the Self with the personality—the folly of seeking to nourish the Soul with gross material food; and how, moreover, it developes, or rather tends to develope, true faith and devotion, and awakens the higher Reason and the Love of the Divine.

* * *

FROM the highest to the lowest, life is

an alternation between rest and motion, between light and darkness, between pleasure and pain. So never allow your heart to sink into despair or to be carried away by any adverse current of thought. You have proved to yourself intellectually, and are now actually experiencing, the shadowy, unreal character of things perceptible by the organs of sense or even by the mind, and the ephemeral nature of all physical and emotional enjoyments. Hold fast, therefore, to the path which will bring you to a view of the real life, however rugged the regions through which it leads, however destitute of joy the deserts across which it now and then winds. Above all, have faith in the Merciful Ones, our Wise Masters, and devote yourself heart and soul to Their service, and all will come out well.

* * *

ALL that is needed for the weeding out of any vice is :

(1) An accurate knowledge of the vice itself;

(2) A recognition—a keen feeling, that it is a *vice*, that it is foolish to entertain it, and that it is worthless; and, lastly,

(3) The will to "kill it out."

This *will* will penetrate into the subconscious sphere where the vice dwells, and slowly but surely erase it.

*
* *

Real tranquillity of mind is never the product of indifference and nonchalance, but can only proceed from an insight into higher and deeper wisdom.

*
* *

A disciple, however humble, of Their High Lodge, has to live in the Eternal, and his life must be a life of Universal Love, or else he must abandon his higher aspirations. The active service which every disciple has to do to the world is different for different classes of students, and is determined by the peculiar nature, disposition, and capacity of the individual. You of course know that, so long as perfection is not achieved, variety has to be maintained even in the mode of service a chelâ must render.

* * *

It is simply impossible to over-estimate the efficacy of Truth in all its phases and bearings in helping the onward evolution of the human Soul. We must love Truth, seek Truth, and live Truth; and thus alone can the Divine Light, which is Truth Sublime, be seen by the student of Occultism. Where there is the slightest leaning towards falsehood in any shape there is shadow and ignorance, and their child, pain. And this leaning towards falsehood belongs to the lower personality without doubt. It is here that our interests clash, it is here that the struggle for existence is in full sway, and it is therefore here that cowardice and dishonesty and fraud find any scope.

THE "signs and symptoms" of the operation of this lower self can never remain concealed from one who sincerely loves Truth and seeks Truth and has devotion to the Great Ones at the foundation of his conduct. Unless the heart be perverse, doubts as to the righteousness of any particular act will never fail to find articulation, and then the true disciple will ask himself: "Will my Master be pleased if I do such and such a thing?" or, "Was it at His bidding that I moved in this way?" And the true answer will soon come up, and then he will learn to mend his ways and harmonise his wishes with the Divine Will and thereafter attain to wisdom and peace.

*
* *

THEOSOPHY is not a thing which can be thrust and hammered *nolens volens* into anybody's head or heart. It must be assimilated with ease in the natural course of evolution, and inhaled like the air around us. Otherwise it will cause indigestion, to use a vulgar expression.

* * *

BEGINNING to feel the growth of one's Soul, one realises the calm that no outward events seem to touch. This, again, is the best proof of spiritual development, and one who feels this, however slightly and vaguely, need not care for any Occult phenomena. From the very beginning of my novitiate I have been taught to rely more upon the calm within than upon any phenomena on the physical, astral, or spiritual planes. And, given favourable conditions and strength in oneself, the less one sees of phenomena, the easier it is to make real and substantial spiritual progress. So my humble advice to you is to devote your attention ever to growing calm within, and not to wish to know in detail the process by which the growth is effected. If you are patient, pure and devoted, you will know all in time, but remember always that perfect and resigned contentment is the soul of spiritual life.

* * *

SPIRITUAL progress is not always the same as goodness and self-sacrifice, although these must in due season bring about the former.

* * *

IT is true that there is in the desire to win the affection of people around one, a tinge of personality which, if eliminated, would make one an angel; but one has to remember that for a long, long time to come our actions will continue to be tinged slightly with a feeling of "self." It must be our constant endeavour to kill this feeling as far as possible, but so long as "self" must show itself in some way, it is much better that it should exist as an inappreciable factor in conduct which is gentle, affectionate and conducive to general welfare, than that the heart should be hardened, the general character rendered angular, the "self" manifesting itself in far less attractive and lovely colours. By this I do not for a moment suggest that efforts should not be made in washing out this faint stain, but what I mean to convey is that the soft and lovely drapery in which the mind clothes itself should not be cast into the fire, simply because it is not one of immaculate whiteness. We have to bear in mind that all our actions are more or less the result of two factors, a desire for self-gratification, and a wish to benefit the world—and our constant effort should be to attenuate as far as is possible the former element, since it may not, till the germ of personality ceases to exist, be completely eliminated. That germ can be killed by processes which the disciple learns as he progresses, by devotion and good actions.

*
* *

THE Masters are always near those of Their servants who by complete self-abnegation have devoted themselves body, mind, and soul to Their service. And even a kind word to these does not go unrequited. In times of severe trial They, in accordance with a beneficent law, let the disciple fight his or her own battle without help from Them; but any-one who encourages Their servant to stand firm has his reward without a doubt.

* * *

KEEPING serene and passionless, there is no doubt that, as the days pass by, one is coming more and more within that influence which is the essence of life, and some day the disciple will be surprised to find he has grown wonderfully without knowing and perceiving the process of growth. For truly the Soul, in its true blooming, "grows like the flower, unconsciously," but gaining in sweetness and beauty by imbibing the sunshine of Spirit.

A COMBATIVE loyalty to any person or cause is hardly commendable in a disciple, and is certainly no indication of spiritual progress.

* * *

THE first step, in almost every case, has the effect of disturbing a nest of hornets. All the odd items of your evil Karma crowd around you thick and fast, and would make one with less steady feet feel giddy and shaky. But one, whose whole object is to lay down, if it need be, his life for the sake of others, without caring for self, has nothing to fear. The very jolting in the ups and downs of this vortex of miseries and trials gives one strength and confidence. and forces the growth of the Soul.

* * *

REMEMBER that the suffering a disciple has to undergo is an integral portion of his training, and flows out of his desire to crush the personality in him. And, at the end, he will find the flower of his Soul blooming the more charmingly for the storm it has braved, and the love and mercy of the Master more than compensating for all he has suffered and sacrificed. It is only a trial for the moment, because at the end he will find he has sacrificed nothing and gained all.

*
* *

LOVE on the highest plane reposes on the serene heights of joy alone, and nothing can cast a shadow on its snowy eminence.

*
* *

PITY and compassion are the proper feelings to cherish in respect to all erring humanity, and we must not give place to any other emotion, such as resentment, annoyance, or vexation. These latter may not only injure ourselves, but also those against whom we may chance to entertain them, but whom we would fain see bettered and freed from all blunders. As we grow spiritually, our thoughts grow incredibly stronger in dynamic power, and none but those who have actual experience know how even a passing thought of an Initiate finds objective form.

*
* *

It is wonderful how the Powers of the Dark seem to sweep away, as it were, in one gust all one's richest spiritual treasures, garnered with such pain and care after years of incessant study and experience. It is wonderful, because after all it is an illusion, and you find it to be one so soon as the peace is restored and light dawns upon you again. You see that you have lost nothing—that all your treasures are there, and the storm and the loss are all a chimera.

*
* *

However heart-rending the outlook may at any time be, however gloomy and dreary the state of things, we must not for one single moment give room to despair;

for despair weakens the mind and thus renders us less capable of serving our Masters.

* * *

KNOW for certain that the Lords of Compassion are always watching their true devotees, and never allow honest hearts and earnest seekers for light to remain under an illusion for any length of time; the Wise Lords bring out of even their temporary recessions lessons which serve them in good stead through the rest of their lives.

* * *

IT is simply our ignorance and blindness that give the appearance of strangeness and unintelligibleness to our work. If we come to view things in their true light and in their full and deeper significations, all will appear perfectly just and fair, and the most perfect expression of the highest reason.

THAT there is in the order of manifested existence not a whit more pain and misery than is absolutely necessary for the ends of the highest evolution, follows directly from the law of Justice and Compassion —the law of Karma and the moral government of the Universe. That each act of self-sacrifice on the part of evolving human monads strengthens the hands of the Masters and brings reinforcement, as it were, to the Powers of Goodness will also be made plain ere we are things of the past—at least to a great many of the present race.

* * *

IT would not avail us much if we knew accurately in detail all that was going to happen to us. For we are not concerned with results, and all we should care about is our own duty; so long as the path is clear to us it is of little consequence what comes of the steps we take on this outer plane. It is the inner life that is the real life; and if our faith in the guidance of our Lords be firm, we ought to have no doubt that whatever the appearances in this illusory sphere may be, all shall go well within, and the world shall go forward on its line of evolution. There is comfort enough in this idea, there is blessedness enough in this thought, and this alone should suffice to nerve us to our present duties and stimulate us to further activity and harder work.

* * *

THERE is a great difference between one who knows the spiritual life to be a reality and the man who only babbles about it but perceives it not, who clutches at and grasps for it, but inhales not its fragrant breath nor feels its exquisite touch.

* * *

THERE is far more wisdom in Those who are watching over us than we have any conception of, and if only we can firmly pin our faith on this we shall not fall into any blunders, and shall be sure to avoid much unnecessary and worse than useless worry. For not a few of our mistakes might be traced to excess of anxiety and fear, to overstrung nerves, and even to too much zeal.

* * *

You will now see that whole-hearted devotion is a potent factor in promoting the growth of the Soul, although it be not seen and realised for the moment; and you will not blame me for having told you to leave aside all thought about phenomena and spiritual knowledge, psychic power and abnormal experiences. For in the serene sunlight of peace every flower of the Soul smiles and grows rich in its peculiar radiant dye. And then some day the disciple looks with amazement at the beauty and delicious fragrance of every flower, rejoices, and in the rejoicing knows that the beauty and radiance emanate from the Lord he has served. The process of growth is not the hackneyed detestable article known to dabblers in pseudo-Occultism. It is a thing mysterious; so sweet, so subtle that none may speak of it, but may only *know* by service.

* * *

You have tasted some drops of the ambrosial waters of Peace, and in the tasting have found strength. Know now and for ever that in the calm of the Soul lies real knowledge, and from the divine tranquillity of the heart comes power. Experience of celestial peace and joy is therefore the only true spiritual life, and growth in peace alone means growth of the Soul. The witnessing of abnormal phenomena by the physical senses can but arouse curiosity and not promote growth. Devotion and peace form the atmosphere in which the Soul doth live, and the more you have of those the more life your Soul will possess. Rely always therefore on the experiences of your Higher Self as a test of your own progress, as also of the reality of the spiritual world, and do not attach any importance to physical phenomena which never do, never can, form the source of strength and comfort.

* * *

THE humble and devoted servants of the Masters really form a chain by which each link is held to the Compassionate Ones. The tightness of the hold of one link to the one next in advance to it, therefore implies the strength of the chain which ever draws us up to Them. Hence one should never fall into the popular fallacy of regarding the love which partakes so largely of the divine as a weakness. Even ordinary love, if it be real, deep and selfless, is the highest and purest manifestation of the Higher Self, and if entertained in one's bosom with constancy and desire of self-sacrifice, ultimately brings one to a clearer realisation of the spiritual world than does any other human act or emotion. What then of a love which has for its basis a common aspiration to reach the Throne of God, a joint prayer to suffer for the ignorant and erring humanity, and a mutual pledge to sacrifice one's own happiness and comfort for the better rendering of service to Those who are ever building a bulwark with Their blessings between the terrible forces of evil and the defenceless orphan—Humanity. . . . But the ideas of the world are all distorted by the selfishness and baseness of human nature. If in love there be weakness, I do not know where lies strength. *Real* strength does not consist in strife and opposition, but lies all-potent in love and inner peace. So the man who cares to live and grow must ever love, and suffer for love.

* * *

When has the world, blind in its ignorance and self-conceit, done full justice to its real saviours and most devoted servants? It is enough that one sees, and in that seeing attempts to dispel to what extent may be possible the delusion of the people around one. The wish that everyone should have the eyes to see and to recognise the Power that works for his regeneration must remain unfulfilled, till the present darkness that hangs like a pall obscuring the spiritual vision has been lifted completely.

PEACE TO ALL BEINGS.